MW01206315

ELIJAH
AND THE PRIESTS OF BAAL

WRITTEN BY
JENNIFER TZIVIA MACLEOD

ILLUSTRATED BY
GOCE ILIEVSKI

Elijah and the priests of Baal © 5774/2014 Jennifer Tzivia MacLeod

About the story:

Most of this story comes from the Biblical text (1 Melachim/Kings, verses 16-45).

The tale of Elijah and the melons is well-known in Israel, especially around Haifa and Mount Carmel, but I couldn't find a midrashic or other traditional source for it. My children and I first discovered it in the Hebrew anthology "Meah Sipurim Rishonim" (One Hundred First Stories), collected by Daniella Gardosh and Talma Alyagon.

Unlike in many of my books, I have used the common English versions of most names in this text. I hope these familiar names will help it find the widest possible readership. Substitute the Hebrew name "Eliyahu" if you prefer.

ISBN-13: 978-1500792978

ISBN-10: 1500792977

All Rights Reserved. No part of this publication may be reproduced, stored in a retrieval system, or transmitted, in any form or in any means – by electronic, mechanical, photocopying, recording or otherwise – without prior written permission

לזכר נשמת אבי מורי

יחיא-ל פינחס בן חיים זאב

In loving memory of

Yechiel Pinchas ben Chaim Zev,

my father.

Pinchas is Eliyahu. God said to Pinchas: You have placed peace between Israel and Myself in this world, and so in the future, you will also be the one to place peace between Myself and My children, as is written: "Behold, I am sending you Eliyah the Prophet."

(Midrash Yalkut Shimoni)

"Get up and go north."
It was a deep voice, one Elijah
had heard before. It was
the voice of God,
and he wished it would
go away.
Its tasks were never easy,
and everywhere he went,
he was hated for doing as
God asked.

"Where shall I go?"
Elijah asked.
There was no answer.
He already knew.
"May I take a drink of
water before I go?"
he asked. But again,
there was no answer.
And so, still thirsty,
Elijah went.

Elijah hoped he might find water along the way.

"Go," God had said, in that voice that allowed him no peace. "Go to Carmel." The eternal green mountain. Now home to idols, and growing drier by the day.

Israel was a wild land, split in two, with a king for the south, the loyal Yehoshefat, and a king for the north, the warrior Achav. But while the south was green and moist, the northern kingdom was desperate.

Years had passed without rain. Crops died: fruits, vegetables, grains. And now the Jews were praying to Baal, one of the old idols. Years before, Joshua and his soldiers had destroyed the old idols. But the people in the north had turned again to Baal.

Elijah found precious little water on his way up the coast. A spring here and there, tufts of green peering out from scorched desert.

Which came first? The famine or the idol worship? Elijah thought he knew. But he also knew he didn't want to get in the people's way.

Yes, he believed in God. *Somebody* had to deliver God's message. But did it have to be his job, every single time?

Baal wasn't just any god. He was the god of thunder, of lightning – the most powerful god the old Canaanites knew. He was the people's last chance for rain, or so they thought.

And now, it was Elijah's job to tell them to stop.

Elijah wasn't the only prophet who hadn't wanted to listen to God. The life of a prophet was rarely much fun. Sometimes, it could get you killed.

When times were good, nobody listened. And when times were hard, as they were now with this drought, the people were too desperate to listen.

Coming between the people and their last chance at rain... that could definitely get you killed.

Of course, only God could send rain. And He had stopped the rain because the people weren't taking care of their land as the Torah said they must.

The longtime residents, the ones who had seen the old temples, statues, idols and priests and ceremonies, had convinced the Jews that Baal was stronger.

So they'd built a temple, on Carmel, full of statues to Baal. A temple of thunder and lightning, Elijah had heard.

But the temple was bone dry.

The green mountain was drying up, and God wouldn't send rain until the last traces of Baal were gone from Israel's north.

And that couldn't happen until Elijah got to Carmel.

So far, nothing was going Elijah's way during his three-day hike from the south, with only sips of water and a few edible roots along the way.

It was true, what he'd heard. The north was not the same: a new king, a different flag. Baal wasn't the only idol he'd seen along the way.

And then he came across the farmer with the melons.

At first, he was sure they were a mirage, so ripe, almost bursting with juice on the sun-baked mountainside. Close up, he saw that they were real. Somewhere, the farmer must have found a spring that still flowed.

"May I have one?" he asked the farmer. "Just a little one."

"These?" the farmer said. "These aren't melons. Just rocks."

The farmer, it seemed, already knew who Elijah was.

How had word of his arrival spread faster than he could travel?

Perhaps somebody had raced to Jaffa's port and taken a swift boat north with the news. Perhaps somebody had ridden a donkey over the Galilee hills to Carmel on the coast. Actually, there were many ways that were faster than a thirsty old prophet on foot.

Someone had warned the people that he was coming. This farmer, and probably also the priests of Baal.

A prophet on foot didn't get much respect outside of Jerusalem these days.

It was all King Achav's fault. A Jewish king, but everybody knew he paid the idol-worshipping priests, sent gold to their temples. He never showed his face in Jerusalem anymore.

"Just rocks," said the farmer again, sizing up Elijah's dusty cloak.

"Rocks?" repeated Elijah. "But these are melons; I can see their leaves and roots. May I buy one?"

"No melons here," said the farmer. "When Baal sends rain, melons will grow. Until then, only rocks."

"Rocks?" roared Elijah. "Do you want to see —" he kicked at the nearest melon, "— what a field of rocks looks like?"

As the farmer watched, Elijah kicked one melon, then another, and then all the others. Each melon he kicked turned into a rock, until the whole field was, as the farmer had said, a worthless field of rocks.

Here on Carmel, they already knew he was coming; now they'd know who they were dealing with. Not him, but the One who had sent him.

Elijah fled the farmer's field, puffing and panting. The farmer might chase him at any minute. He thought he heard footsteps pounding in the sand behind him, but he didn't turn. Jackals howled in the distance. He ran until night fell, then took shelter in a cave.

Over a small fire, he baked the last of his flour into little cakes. He wouldn't last long here.

But he had a job to do. How could he convince the stubborn, wild people of this wild northern land that God was the answer to their drought?

Twigs crackled at the cave's entrance. Elijah sat up. Around the corner came a young boy, damp with sweat: the farmer's son. In a rugged bag, which he held out to Elijah, he carried a single, small melon.

"Don't listen to the people here," the boy said. "Some of us still believe."

Carefully, Elijah cut the melon apart to share with the boy. Its juice ran sweetly down his chin, into his beard, onto his robe. He didn't care.

"Will you go back tonight?" Elijah asked.

"I must," he said. "If I am caught outside after dark..." He shuddered.

"You may remain here with me."

"It will be worse for you if I do. No, I will return."

"Thank you," said Elijah, as the boy slipped back out into the night.

The very next morning, Elijah went to the temple of Baal. There was no chance he could convince the people, but maybe if he tried something, God might let him return to Jerusalem in peace.

Two priests met him at the gates.

"Oh, no, old man," one said, wagging a finger.

"This is holy ground," said the other, blocking his way. "Nothing here for you."

Elijah thought for a moment. "Is your god truly in this place?" he asked.

"Of course," said one of the priests.

"And is he more powerful than I?"

Again, the priest laughed. "Of course."

"Then my presence here cannot harm him," said Elijah. And with that, he strolled through the gates. In the dim light inside, Elijah saw statues all around; he could make out golden columns and pillars up and down the hall.

The two priests ran alongside, hurrying to keep up.

"We are Jews, just like you," said one of the priests.

"We have nothing to hide," said the other, following Elijah even deeper inside. He wore a gold robe, a wrapped turban on his head. "We are just trying to save our families. We still believe in God... we only call on Baal to help Him in this time of danger."

To help God! Did these priests really think He needed their help?

Elijah stopped at the golden chamber; the heart of the temple.

"You have come just in time," the golden priest said. "Today we will hold a special sacrifice, to prove to Baal that we deserve his precious rain." He strode over to one of the statues a few paces away.

"And then," whispered the other to Elijah, "we will return to worshipping God, when the danger has passed."

Just as Elijah had heard, the temple was full of thunder: distant rumbles made by the priests with metal sheets to convince their god to send the real thing.

And just as he had heard, the temple was full of lightning: paintings of lightning, and flashes of fire, bouncing off mirrors waved by priests over flames in the temple's inner depths.

Nothing was real inside the temple except the people's hope; a hope that they and their families could survive the drought.

And somehow, also, the hope that they could return to God's love once again. But how could that happen in the midst of this great Baal frenzy?

"Bring in the sacrifice!" called the golden priest.

In marched two more priests. Between them squirmed a young boy, trying to break free.

It was the farmer's son.

A crowd had gathered, chanting: "Bring the rain! Bring the rain!" A priest approached the boy with a knife as he was led to a great, stone altar in the middle of the hall.

"Stop!" screamed Elijah. Everybody turned. "How long will you all go back and forth? Pretending to believe in God, while serving this... this idol!"

The people murmured; a few shrugged. The priest standing beside the wriggling boy held his knife.

"Wait!" yelled Elijah. "This is not what Baal wants. He will never send rain if you do the sacrifice here, inside this filthy, dark temple."

The golden priest appeared at his side. "Suddenly, you are an expert on Baal? So tell me. What does he want, then?"

"A fair fight," said Elijah. "Outside. Two altars, one for Baal, one for God. A test between two gods, to prove once and for all who is more powerful."

The priest stood in thought for a minute. He smiled and nodded. To the other priests, he called, "bring stones and build a new altar – outside, on the mountain. And then... bring the boy!"

Elijah shook his head. "That will never work, offering the boy. Since God only accepts sacrifices of kosher animals, Baal must do the same for their contest to be fair. The sacrifices must be identical."

"Of course," said the priest, after a moment. "Bring a bull – no, bring *two* bulls! But hold onto the boy as well, just in case."

For hours, the priests built their altar. As they ran past, perhaps four hundred of them, with stones and buckets of sand and mortar, Elijah labored alone under the hot sun.

"What are you waiting for, old man?" a priest sneered. "Build your altar! How can God win without even one faithful servant to build Him an altar?"

Elijah struggled to gather and bring back stones, laying them on the ground in the shape of an altar's base. But each stone grew heavier and heavier as the sun rose mercilessly into the sky.

Just as the sun had passed its peak, just as Elijah's hands were slick with sweat, and about to drop the stone he carried, a shadow fell over him.

A boy, not much older than the one who'd visited last night, bent under the weight of a heavy stone. Behind him, there was another boy, and another, all carrying stones. Perhaps a dozen of them, young and eager to help.

And the stones they carried – they were the size and shape of melons.

With bags and bags of sand, the boys stacked their large stones onto and around Elijah's foundation. With mud and clay, they forced them into place. And just before the sun set over the western sea, bringing darkness and a merciful breeze, God's altar was complete.

The boys slipped away, and Elijah returned to his cave, where he lay, half-dozing all night, dreading what would happen in the morning.

Morning came slowly, but when it did, Elijah returned to the altars. A crowd had gathered. There, at the front, stood King Achav. He must have summoned all these people to witness Elijah's humiliation.

They all stared.

Heads turned, first to him, then to the king. And nearby, the two altars. Everybody waited for something to happen.

The fierceness that had overtaken him when he kicked the melons flooded Elijah again and he shouted to the crowd.

"How long can you go back and forth?" he yelled once again. "Offering sacrifices here, there, everywhere? When will you understand that it is only God who can save you? We will see today who is truly powerful, the God of Abraham, Isaac and Jacob... or your god of stone and gold and fakery."

A silence descended, but only for a moment.

Then, the king's impatient voice rang out. "Bring the bulls!"

Two altars, and two bulls.

The bulls were identical, as far as Elijah could tell.

"You choose first," he said, with a wave of his hand to the priests. "Choose the one your god will love best."

As the priests led their chosen bull away, Elijah saw that it was indeed just a little taller, straighter, and heavier. A fine bull.

Elijah called to the crowd. "Two bulls! Two altars! But only one true God. These men will lay their bull on their altar, and I shall lay mine here. But none of us shall touch fire to the wood. Any god who desires his bull must set it alight himself!"

For three hours, Elijah struggled with the bull. It had been tied for him, but the slaughter, the rituals with its blood, the butchering — it all took time. Normally, it was the kohanim, from the tribe of Levi, who prepared the animals in Jerusalem. But nothing here was normal, and so it fell to Elijah himself, who was not nearly as young as he used to be.

His strength was nearly gone.

At last, Elijah's bull was laid out on the altar. He looked up and realized that the Baal priests had been finished for hours, and the mood in the crowd was like a party: the priests were passing wine around in jars and skins, and the entire crowd was chanting, calling on Baal to set fire to their bull.

"Hear us, Baal!" the priests cried. The crowd, giddy and drunk, roared together, "Hear us!"

The priests hopped and danced around their altar. They chanted. Some wailed, cried, and threw their bodies at the stones. Nothing happened.

One of the priests walked up and cut himself, dropping his own blood onto the bull on the altar for Baal. Nothing happened. Another priest came and did the same, and then another.

Each time, the crowd groaned with disappointment. Slowly, they put down their flasks of wine. The insistent drumbeats slowed and the pipe music ground down as they realized nothing was happening. Baal was not answering.

"Your god is too busy, perhaps?" called Elijah. "Perhaps he is on a journey... or sleeping?"

And at this, the crowd actually laughed.

"Draw near!" called Elijah. Incredibly, the crowd gathered around him now, close to God's altar.

"Bring water!" he cried. Buckets appeared at his side. Once, twice, ignoring his own thirst, he poured the precious water, filling the trench he had dug all around his altar, and then, to the gasps of the crowd, all over his bull.

He heard the whispers. "How can it burn?" "The old man is crazy!"

But in the crowd also, there was hope. "Perhaps... perhaps..."

"God!" he called, his voice cracking. "God! I have done as you asked. You have sent me here to these people, the children of Abraham, of Isaac, of Jacob. They have turned their backs on you, but you – you are full of infinite forgiveness. Forgive them, and lead them back to You."

And then – there was silence.

Not a person spoke in the crowd.

Not a raven cawed in the treetops.

Not a cat purred in the temple.

Nothing happened.

The Baal priest in the golden robe slipped up alongside Elijah.

"Now we see," he whispered with a hiss, his breath musty with wine. He grinned, ready to declare victory.

The golden priest stepped closer to the altar. He spat on Elijah's bull. Carefully slaughtered, prepared, laid out for God.

And with that, it ignited, bursting into flames which caught the priest's robe and sent him screaming down the hill. "Fire!" he yelled.

The crowd fell on their faces.

"The Lord, He is God! The Lord, He is God!" they cried, over and over and over.

Faces in the once-dry dust, turned muddy from the tears streaming down their cheeks.

Elijah stretched his arms towards heaven, surrounded by the crowd of Jews. Almost carried alive to heaven by their chants and prayers.

But he would not leave them now – not yet.

These were his people, and he must remain with them a while longer.

God was not finished with Elijah yet, he knew.

He looked down at these hundreds, thousands of stubborn people – until seconds ago, willing to place their fate in the hands of a powerless idol. And now, swaying together in the smoke and steam, utterly convinced of God's might.

He knew they would turn away from Him again and again. In that triumphant moment, he foresaw their long exile ahead, the thousands of years scattered among the nations.

Even amid the joy of his people, he mourned their future.

Then, he looked upward. Almost hidden by the heavy smoke that filled the air, a tiny black cloud drifted into sight. And then, drops of rain began to fall on the steaming, parched earth.

To cries of joy, the barren land returned to life once again.

And the tired old prophet tilted his head back, laughed, and drank in the rain drops pouring down his face.

About the Author:

Jennifer Tzivia MacLeod is the proud mother of four (two big and two little). She lives near Haifa, and loves learning more about Israel and its stories.

Visit her at http://www.Tzivia.com

About the Illustrator:

Goce Ilievski is an award-winning artist who lives and works in Skopje, Macedonia. In addition to several previous children's books, his paintings have been exhibited in group and solo exhibitions. Reach him at goce_i@hotmail.com.

Can you help me out?

As a self-publishing writer, I don't have a big company promoting my books. I depend on readers like you to leave feedback so I can keep sharing stories. If you and your kids enjoyed this book, please take a minute to let others know.

Thank you!